Lexile

Ø

A Calf Is Born

Kiyonori Kaizuki

translated from the Japanese by Cathy Hirano

ORCHARD BOOKS • New York

On a cold winter night the sun has set, and shadows spread over snow and sky. The lights in the farmhouse come on.

A full moon rises beside the barn.

Climbing high in the sky, the moon casts a
pale light on the wall.

From within the dimly lit barn, a sound can be heard—it is the painful lowing of a cow about to give birth.

The mother cow pushes hard to help her calf.
Her breathing comes in gasps, and the sound
of her lowing carries far into the night.
Suddenly the calf's head appears.

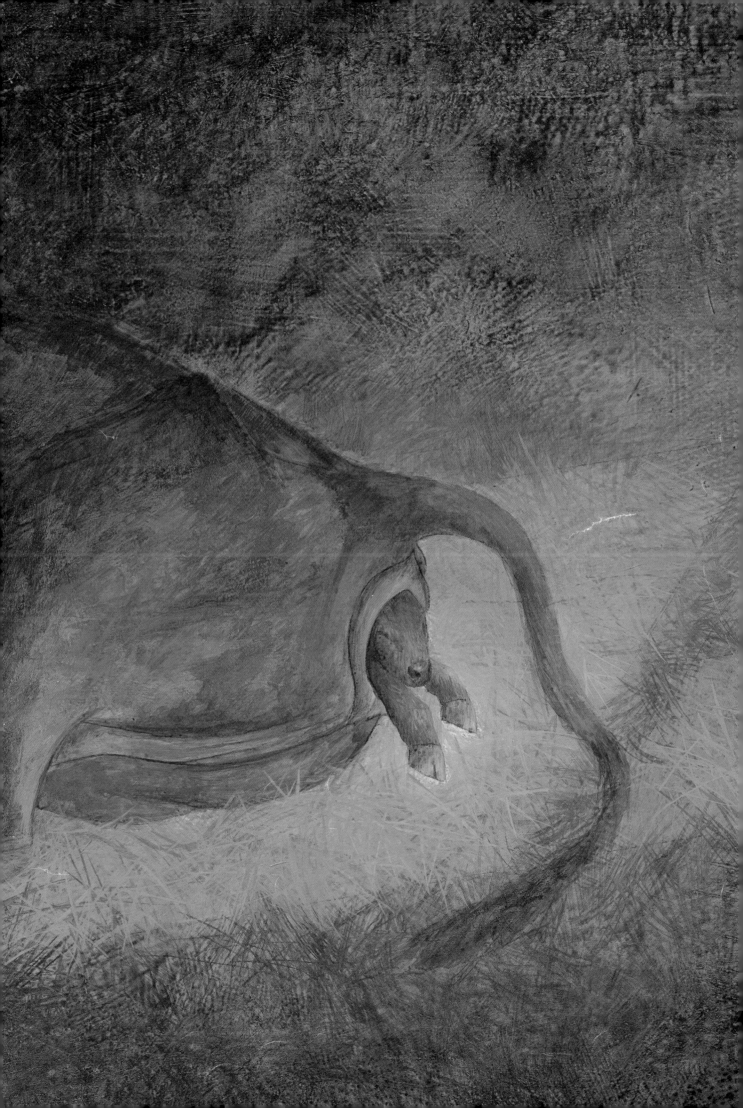

As the first rays of sunlight pour through the window, the calf is born. The mother is exhausted, but she starts to lick her calf right away, helping to remove the thin film that protected him before he was born.

Soon the calf tries to stand up by himself. He wobbles and totters, trying again and again. His mother watches closely. The calf nudges against her, searching for milk. When he finds her udder, he drinks until he is full.

Finally the calf stands by himself and goes outside for the very first time.

Outside, there are many other cows, all eating hungrily.

Spring is on its way, but patches of snow still cover the ground.

Later on, something seems wrong with the calf. He curls up on the straw, shivering. His nose is running, and he seems listless and weak.

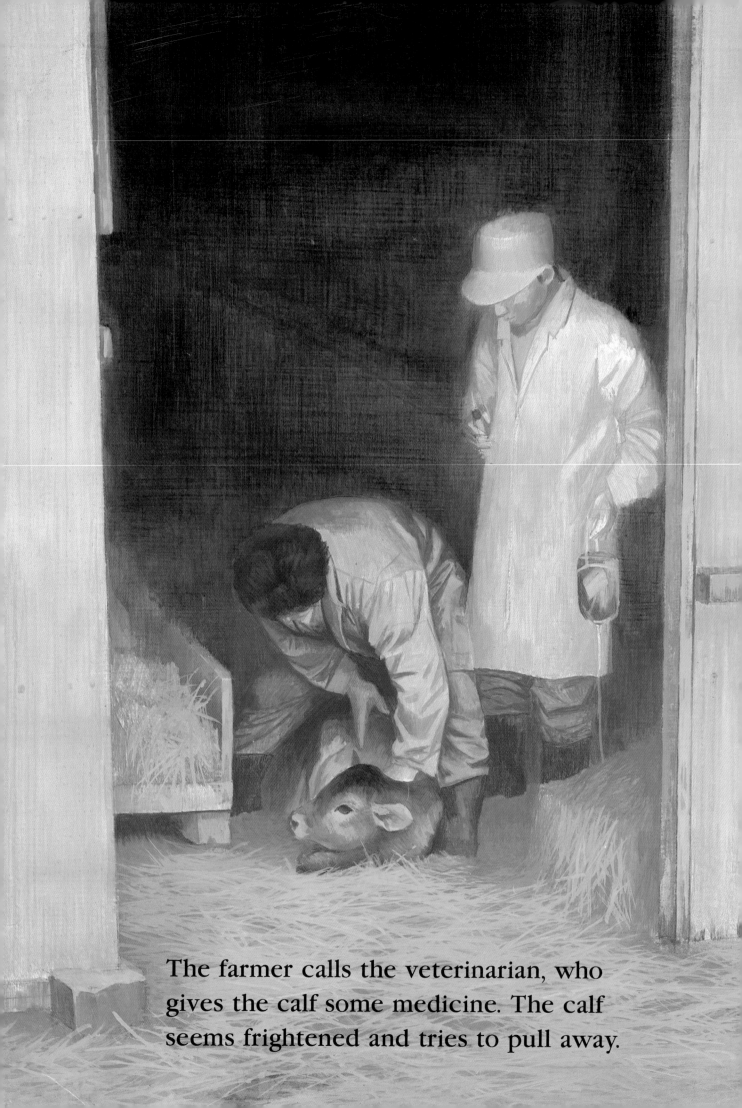

The farmer calls the veterinarian, who gives the calf some medicine. The calf seems frightened and tries to pull away.

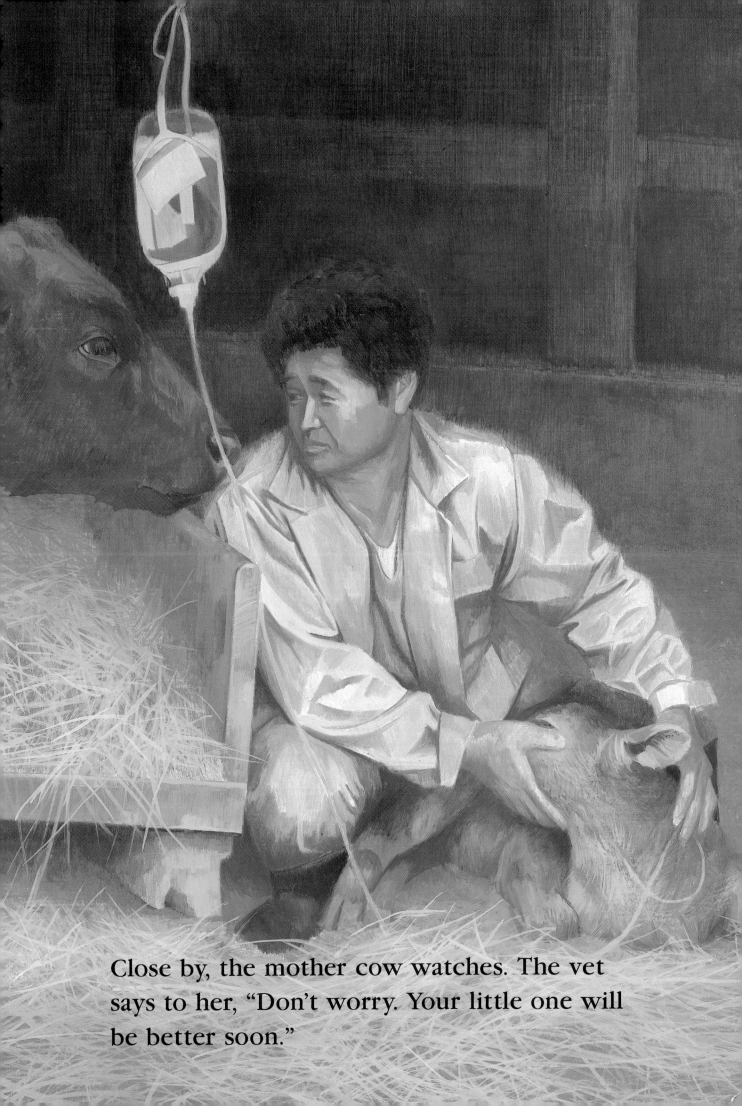

Close by, the mother cow watches. The vet says to her, "Don't worry. Your little one will be better soon."

The little calf does recover quickly. Tugging at his mother, he drinks greedily once again.

Now that his stomach is full, he wants to play. Everything the calf sees is new to him!

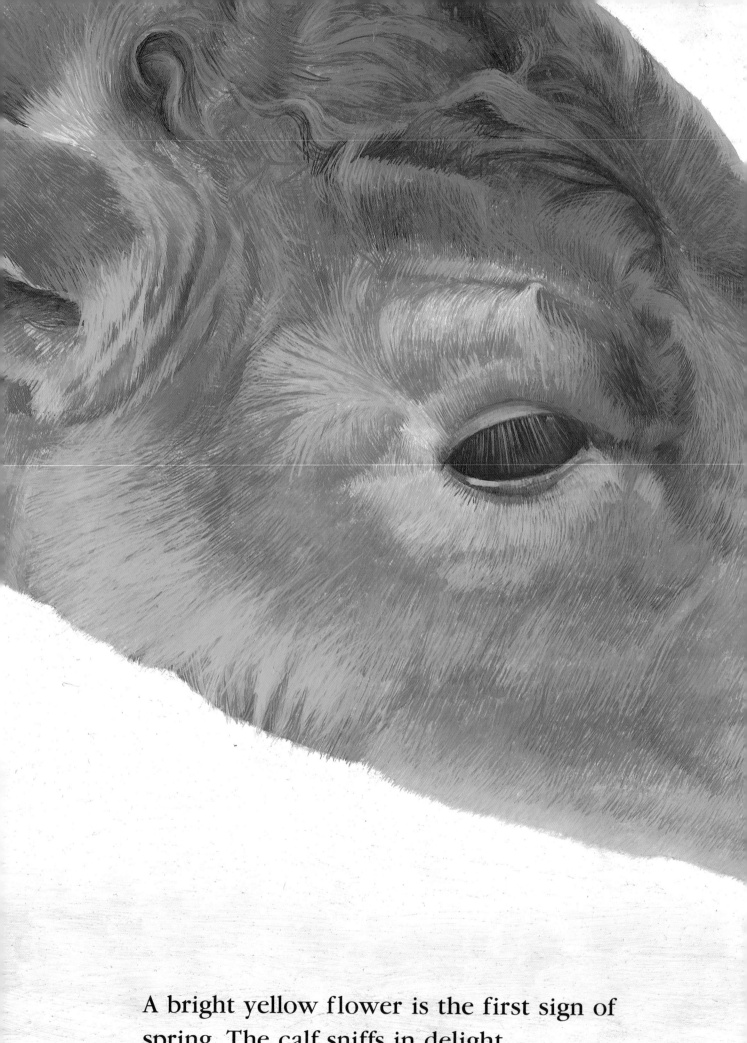

A bright yellow flower is the first sign of spring. The calf sniffs in delight.

Nearby, some
young steers are
chewing noisily. The
little calf walks up to take a
closer look at what they are eating.

After eating, the steers lie down on the straw
to relax in the sun. The little calf goes in
search of his mother.

In the late afternoon, the cow and her newborn nuzzle together.

The farmer walks them back to the
barn as the sky turns a pale pink.

When evening arrives, the little calf is back in
the barn with his mother, sleeping peacefully
after his first day on the farm.

Originally published in Japan in 1988 under the title *Koushi Ga Umaretayo (A Calf Was Born)* by Fukutake Publishing
Co., Ltd., Tokyo, Japan
Copyright © 1988 by Kiyonori Kaizuki
Based on an English translation by Cathy Hirano arranged through Fukutake Publishing Co., Ltd.
First American Edition 1990 published by Orchard Books
English language translation copyright © 1990 by Orchard Books

ORCHARD BOOKS
A division of Franklin Watts, Inc.
387 Park Avenue South
New York, NY 10016

Manufactured in the United States of America
Printed by General Offset Company, Inc.
Bound by Horowitz/Rae
Book design by Jean Krulis

10 9 8 7 6 5 4 3 2 1

The text of this book is set in 20 pt. Garamond Book.
The illustrations are oil paintings.

Library of Congress Cataloging-in-Publication Data

Kaizuki, Kiyonori.
    [Koushi ga umareta yo. English]
    A calf is born / Kiyonori Kaizuki ; translated from the Japanese
by Cathy Hirano.
        p. cm.
    Translation of: Koushi ga umareta yo.
    Summary: Describes the birth of a calf one cold winter night and
his first day of life as he learns to stand, ventures out of doors,
and nuzzles up to his tired mother.
    ISBN 0−531−05862−X. ISBN 0−531−08462−0 (lib. bdg.)
    1. Calves—Juvenile literature. 2. Cattle—Parturition—Juvenile
literature. [1. Cattle. 2. Birth.] I. Title
SF197.5.K3513 1990
636.2′07—dc20   89−23091
                                                      CIP
                                                      AC